WIDOWS' AND ORPHANS' EDITION.

MAJ. R. ADNERSON,

U. S. A.

Marula

An imprint of Arcadia Publishing

Within Fort Sumter
A View of Major Anderson's Garrison Family for One Hundred and Ten Days
by Miss A. Fletcher

A Marula Historical Reprint
Originally published in 1861

Published by Arcadia Publishing
Charleston SC

ISBN 978-0-7385-9495-8

Printed in the United States of America

For all general information contact Arcadia Publishing at:
Telephone 843-853-2070
Fax 843-853-0044
E-mail sales@arcadiapublishing.com
For customer service and orders:
Toll-Free 1-888-313-2665

Visit us on the Internet at www.arcadiapublishing.com

WITHIN FORT SUMTER;

OR,

A VIEW OF MAJOR ANDERSON'S GARRISON FAMILY FOR ONE HUNDRED AND TEN DAYS.

BY ONE OF THE COMPANY.

(Miss A. Fletcher)

NEW YORK:
N. TIBBALS & COMPANY,
120 NASSAU STREET, (UP STAIRS).

1861.

ELECTROTYPED BY
SMITH & McDOUGAL,
82 & 84 Beeekman-st.

WITHIN FORT SUMTER.

WITHIN! Did you ever reflect how much, of which you know nothing, that word contains? Of all that is presented to your eye you only see the exterior: of the *within* you are ignorant. Conjecture says a great deal, but who *knows* what is within the ocean's bosom—what is within the earth's crust—what is within the human heart? You meet your fellow man, you see the motion of his limbs, the play of his features, the glance of his eyes; but you can not tell what is occupying his mind.

This train of thinking was induced by the many reports that were circulated while Major Anderson and his little band lay imprisoned in the Island Fortress of Charleston Bay. Even in what was passing outside and around, of which the public eye had range, Rumor contradicted herself; but, of what transpired *within* that wave-washed stronghold, prying conjecture was completely at fault.

All is over now—the peril, the anxiety, the conflict—the result is known; and the details which led to that result—the inner works, upon which speculation so persistently blundered, may as well be known also.

In December 1860, when the State of South Carolina desired to secede from the Federal Union, Major Anderson, of the 1st Regiment of U. S. Artillery, was in command of the forts of Charleston harbor; and, with his company, was stationed at Fort Moultrie, on Sullivan's Island. He saw the spreading commotion; and—as a Sea-Captain, in stormy weather, glass in hand, sweeping the horizon with his eye, uninterested in natural wonders or scientific questions, is wholly engrossed with the care and management of his ship—he thought not of political affairs, but studied only his duty as a servant of the Republic—an officer of the American Army.

Situated as he then was, he found himself utterly weak in case of an attack—his fort was insecure, his garrison was small—he, therefore, petitioned Government for more troops; but received for reply that, as the movement would increase disaffection, the Administration preferred not granting his request unless necessitated. He now looked round him, with a view to strengthening his position, as best he could. On a point of James Island, facing Fort Moultrie, west by south, stood Fort Johnson, and between these, nearly in mid channel, an artificial Island had been raised, on which a fortification was built, now in course of completion; and here, with the waters to wall him in, and the shores all round the bay under range of his guns, Major Anderson decided to concentrate his little force.

The island fort was now occupied by Captain Foster, of the Engineer department, who was engaged in finishing its internal arrangements, mounting its heavy ordnance, &c., and Major Anderson urged him to hasten with the important work.

On the 20th of December, a State Convention, then assembled in Charleston, unanimously resolved on secession, and, on the 24th of that month the Declaration of South Carolina, withdrawing herself from the Federal Union, was publicly announced and acted upon. The excitement among the Revolutionists was intense, Fort Moultrie was in danger of attack, and, Captain Foster reporting to Major Anderson the fitness of Fort Sumter for occupation, measures were immediately taken to effect a silent and speedy removal.

On Wednesday evening, the 26th of December, just after sun-set, three little schooners, with four or five barges, were anchored under the walls of Fort Moultrie; and the little company were busily engaged in the work of transferring their effects on board. The Surgeon, with all the essentials of his office, and the Hospital furniture, were moved first; then the women, with their children and household treasures; next went the light arms and ammunition—the soldiers and their equipments; and last the officers, who, all through that night, had stood around their Commander, as true and brave men always do in hours of emergency.

The flight was effected without discovery;

though a watch had been posted at either side of the bay to observe their movements, as well as to look out for, and prevent the entrance of, re-enforcements. A friendly haze had filled the atmosphere, under whose cover the little fleet had sped; and "the watchman watched in vain."

Major Anderson, before leaving Fort Moultrie, had spiked the cannon, destroyed the carriages, and cut down the flag staff; and the only regret expressed or felt was that the fort could not be blown up.

Next morning the mist cleared away, the sun arose, and showed to Charleston and its surroundings the United States Flag floating proudly over Fort Sumter, and Fort Moultrie sitting in deserted gloom. Captain Foster, with a few of his men, had been left in the latter fort; but on its being taken possession of, as it immediately was, by the Revolutionists, he took boat and withdrew to Fort Sumter. A few hours and the Palmetto flag waved over Fort Moultrie, Castle Pinkney, and, in Charleston, over the Custom House, Post Office and U. S. Arsenal.

In the afternoon the Governor of the State addressed a letter to Major Anderson requesting to be informed whether the step he had just taken was by the order of his Government or upon his own responsibility; and received for reply that the Major's recent act was his own, without any instructions from Government: he being in command of all the forts in that harbor occupied them at his discretion.

The day following Major Anderson received the following dispatch, through telegraph, from the Secretary of War:

"It is rumored here that you have spiked your guns, burned your carriages and moved to Fort Sumter. If so, you have violated your orders. Answer immediately."

To which the Major replied,

"The rumor is correct that I spiked my guns, burned my carriages, and moved my command to Fort Sumter. I did so in the discharge of my duty."

But Secretary Floyd's censure was not coincided with by the Administration; Major Anderson's course was not only justified, but approved.

Meanwhile the Commander of Fort Sumter is busily preparing for expected action. All is activity within the stronghold; the men engaged in strengthening defenses and mounting guns, the women in arranging the quarters. The latter soon discovered that the sudden and hasty removal had not been without inconvenience, in a pecuniary sense,—furniture and clothes had been damaged, and small valuables lost; but there was no murmuring. To one couple the loss amounted to two hundred dollars' worth; but the wife smiled as she remarked:

"We have one another yet, though, thank God."

All honor to such soldiers' wives! May the country never supply to her fighting sons any less worthy!

The single men had less to lose, but they fared no better, for their barrack contained only empty walls. Bunks were put up, into which shavings were thrown, to serve as beds; and rude, and hastily constructed tables and benches completed the furniture; but, brave fellows, no thought of personal discomfort mingled with their deep sympathy in their commander's stern and trying position, and the all pervading feeling of every heart was the manly determination to do their whole duty to the last.

And so they worked heartily, day after day, more securely fortifying their stronghold; and feeling confident in its capacity for either resistance or attack, whichever might be demanded of it. Upreared from the water it was only assailable by a fleet; and the outer wall, of solid, concrete masonry, twelve feet in thickness and sixty feet in hight, bid bold defiance to invading force. It was pierced for one hundred and forty guns, but was not furnished with much more than half that number. These, however, were mounted and placed in the most salient points, looking formidably forth on the surrounding scene, able and willing for effective work.

Nor was the busy garrison unobservant of what was going on outside. They could see the Secessionists, also at work, restoring Fort Moultrie and building batteries. And O! how they longed to open the mouths of their cannon upon them, and put an end to preparations which, they knew, were intended for their own injury! But no warlike demonstration would Major Anderson make, so long as the other party were willing to remain at peace; besides that he had hopes of a favorable termination of the difficulty being effected in Washington.

For some time the Major was kept ignorant of the views and purposes of the War Department—despatches not being committed to the mail lest they should be opened in Charleston. There might be re-enforcements sent to him, he knew not, he could only wait, and while waiting do the best his situation afforded. The approach of re-enforcements the Revolutionists also anticipated, and placed a force at Morris Island to prevent their entrance.

In this anxious and clouded state of affairs the New Year opened upon the little garrison at Fort Sumter. A few days, however, brought a cheering visit from the wife and the brother of the commander. O! those family ties—those sweet, home affections! what would life be without them?—all drudgery—no respite; all storm—no calm; all rough, thorny walking—no smooth, soft stopping place; all cold, and hard, and bitter, without one soothing, mollifying charm—O! thank God for love!

At last, on Wednesday morning, January 9, the long-looked-for succor appeared: a steamer bearing the American flag, was approaching. The garrison were in ecstacy: but their joy was soon turned to indignation, for scarcely had the vessel entered the waters of the harbor, when the revolutionary batteries opened fire upon her. The time for action seemed to have come now; and every man rushed to his post, ready for the word of command. But the word came not. The Major stood on the rampart, the glass to his eye, scanning the scene, until the steamer, shocked and insulted at her rude reception, turned and put back to sea. Then the Major descended, retired to his apartment, and wrote a letter, which he deputed Lieutenant Hall to bear to the Governor.

The boat with its white flag departed, while excitement reigned through the garrison. The men—even the women were wild with impatience to avenge the affront put upon their country's flag. A United States vessel fired into and the daring act unpunished! It required all the authority of the officers to keep the guns from speaking: it took all their affection for, and all their faith in the judgment of their commander to keep the men still, while the women urgently offered their own assistance. One fair enthusiast bared her white arm, and, with a friction tube in her fingers, sprung to a gun, declaring she would fire it herself. She was a tall, young, bright-looking woman; a fine specimen of proud Virginia's daughters.

"You have a great deal of courage," said Captain Doubleday, as he gently drew her back from the gun.

"Courage!" she exclaimed—and her form became erect, and her eye lighted up,—"I should think, Sir, a soldier's wife *ought* to have courage!"

This lady's husband, John H. Davis, was a Marylander; and here we may mention that of all the loyal hearts in that loyal little band, none beat more truly than those of natives of Southern States.

Arrived at the Governor's head-quarters, Lieutenant Hall requested an interview, which, being immediately granted, he presented the letter of his chief, and awaited a reply.

The letter was as follows:

"*To his Excellency the Governor of South Carolina.*

"SIR:—Two of your batteries fired this morning on an unarmed vessel bearing the flag of my Government. As I have not been notified that war has been declared by South Carolina against the United States, I can not but think this a hostile act committed without your sanction or authority. Under that hope I refrain from opening a fire on your batteries. I have the honor, therefore, respectfully to ask whether the above mentioned act—one which, I believe, is without parallel in the history of our country, or any other civilized government—was committed in obedience to your instructions, and notify you, if it is not disclaimed, that I regard it as an act of war. And I shall not, after reasonable time for the return of my messenger, permit any vessel to pass within the range of the guns of my fort.

"In order to save, as far as it is in my power, the shedding of blood, I beg you will take due notification of my decision for the good of all concerned. Hoping, however, your answer may justify a further continuance of forbearance on my part,

"I remain, respectfully,

"ROBERT ANDERSON.

"FORT SUMTER, January 9, 1861."

Governer Pickens, in reply, stated the position of South Carolina to the United States, and said that any attempt to send United States troops to re-enforce Major Anderson, or to re-take the forts of South Carolina, was regarded by the authorities of the State, as an act of coërcion on the part of the United States Government. Due notice of this was sent to all approaching vessels; and the Star of the West, despite of warning, having entered the harbor with troops, was, consequently, fired into.

With this answer Lieutenant Hall retired. An escort conducted him to his boat, and he sped back to Fort Sumter, where Major Anderson paced to and fro, under a grave consciousness of weighty responsibility.

Upon receiving the Governor's reply Major

Anderson decided upon a course which for the last hour had been revolving in his mind. He determined to have instructions from Washington. He therefore desired his first Lieutenant to prepare for a journey thither, at the same time directing the Captain to order the men to retire from the guns, as no action would be taken at present.

The same afternoon the boat and white flag again left Fort Sumter for Charleston, bearing Lieutenant Talbott, with the following letter.

"*To his Excellency the Governor of South Carolina.*

"SIR:—I have the honor to acknowledge the receipt of your communication, and say that under the circumstances I have deemed it proper to refer the whole matter to my Government; and intend deferring the course indicated in my note this morning until the arrival from Washington of such instructions as I may receive.

"I have the honor also to express the hope that no obstructions will be placed in the way, and that you will do me the favor of giving every facility for the departure and return of the bearer, Lieutenant T. Talbott, who is directed to make the journey.

"I remain, respectfully,

"ROBERT ANDERSON.

"FORT SUMTER, January 9, 1861."

Governor Pickens expressed his polite acquiescence in the request of Major Anderson, and immediately directed that every facility be afforded Lieutenant Talbott to prosecute his journey, and every courtesy be extended to him, as the bearer of dispatches.

These dispatches contained a statement of affairs at Fort Sumter, an account of the reception of the Star of the West, and an entreaty for instructions.

About this time rumors got afloat of disaffection and mutiny among the soldiers of the fort; and the indignant blood rushed to the honest cheek of every man and woman of the little band as they read, in the newspapers, these cruel and injurious calumnies. They thirsted, more than ever, for an opportunity to display their staunch devotion to the cause of Government. Before their bravery was to be tested, now their honor was to be vindicated; and each heart panted for the hour when, either with their arms or their lives, they should wipe out the treacherous falsehood.

This feeling pervaded the whole company; and when, on the 11th of January, commissioners from Charleston, under a flag of truce, came to Major Anderson to demand the surrender of the fort, the reply was,

"We will fire the Magazine, and be buried in one common ruin, before we will surrender!"

The sentiment was echoed by loud and prolonged cheers from every voice in the garrison.

What use to propose base terms to such men?

Still under the hope, however, of a peaceable adjustment of the national difference, Major Anderson consented to unite with South Carolina in sending a deputation to Washington to ask the evacuation of Fort Sumter; and, accordingly, on the 12th of January, Lieutenant Hall, on the part of Major Anderson, and Colonel Hayne on that of South Carolina, departed on that mission.

January 18 brought the return of Lieutenant

Talbott, with the reply of the Administration to the despatches of which he had been the bearer; by which the Commander of Fort Sumter was advised that his line of action was highly approved by his Government; that it was decided not to make another attempt at re-enforcing him at present; and also instructing him to suffer no indignities to the American flag,—if any such were again offered, to open his batteries upon the perpetrators.

The want of fuel began to be felt now in the garrison. The weather had been mostly pleasant, so that they had been permitted to use their store with economy; but it would hold out no longer—it must be replenished. With this view a boat containing nine men was sent to shore; but the men were seized and made prisoners. The Governor, however, when made aware of the fact, ordered their discharge.

And now another difficulty—the mails were untrustworthy. Major Anderson remonstrated, when it was proposed to him to send them to Fort Johnson—about half distance southwardly from Charleston to Fort Sumter. But this arrangement did not suit the Major, so he despatched a telegram to Washington on the subject. An immediate reply came, threatening to withdraw the Government support from the Charleston Post Office; but the State was not ready to take that expense into her own hands, and the Fort Sumter mails, therefore, were treated with more respect.

On the 19th January the marketing, with which the garrison had been hitherto supplied, was stopped. Captain Doubleday proceeded to Charleston to enquire the cause of the stoppage, and learned that orders to that effect had been received from the Governor.

Nor yet did this dishearten the little garrison: they had plenty of biscuit, salt-pork, and coffee, and declared they could live well on this fare until the time should come for them to strike a blow for "Uncle Sam."

This cheerful submission of his gallant company to the ills and annoyances of their lot considerably aided Major Anderson in maintaining his difficult post. Yet were not his public trials enough—his tender feelings must also suffer—the 21st of the month brought him a telegram informing him of the illness of his wife. And now, between professional care and private anxiety, the hero of Charleston Harbor enjoys but little repose. His heart palpitating with suspense, while his head still works in the cause of duty; his thoughts straining homeward at the same time that he is inspecting and superintending, with his own eyes, the most minute military detail! O! honor your faithful servants, America! deal kindly with them ever! and, while you sleep on an easy bed, and eat your meat with cheerful appetite, forget not those who stand on your bulwarks—their breasts your shields, their lives your safeguard!

January 23d. The Southern Confederacy became organized. It was no longer the State of South Carolina, with which the Federal Government had to contend, but several States combined. An amicable settlement seemed farther off than ever.

That an attack would soon be made upon Fort Sumter was evident: preparations with that intent were fast progressing; and this consideration, joined to the desire to reduce the consumption of his store of provisions, decided

Major Anderson to send from the fort all but the efficient fighting men.

To the soldiers' wives this was a distressing contingency; but no word, no sign showed an unwillingness to comply with whatever was best under the circumstances. With smothered sighs and suppressed tears the women prepared to depart—very different was the cheerful alacrity with which the same preparation was entered upon a month before: poor things! they left Moultrie *with* their husbands, they left Sumter *without* them.

January 25th the removal took place: the women and children, and such of the workmen as were not willing to serve in a military capacity, left the fort—the strong and brave were alone. Perhaps it should have been written the *stronger* and *braver*, for many a woman and child departed that day who, to the utmost of their ability, would have done and dared as much as their husbands and fathers. This had been seen in all their bearing; and, even in the last hour, when the sobbing farewells were spoken, words of hopeful encouragement were all that flowed from their gentle lips—in not one case did affection breathe the dastardly counsel to self-preservation.

"We have been seven years married," said one, "and I never had reason to find fault with you; now, whatever may happen, I *know* I shall never have cause to blush for you."

"And I don't want you to think of *us*, Ben," said another, though her swollen eyes belied her words; "the children and myself will get along, and you'll have enough to think of *here*."

And another, holding a large, coarse hand between her own, and leaning her head against the brawny shoulder, whispered with quivering lips:

"May God bless, and take care o' you, Thomas,—I'll never cease to pray for you; but do your juty, do your juty, darlint;—God forbid that my love should intherfere with that."

This last, from her tongue, was a child of green Erin; and her husband, Thomas Carroll, did his "juty" well, when the hour for duty came—and carried a wounded *face* away from Fort Sumter.

There was bright and beautiful weather in Charleston Harbor; but the light was all gone from the stronghold over which the American banner waved. What were sparkling waters and gay sunshine to those who had just lost the sweet smile of woman—the merry laugh of childhood? Nothing was around them, or before them, now, but hard, stern service.

And still were propagated those base reports of treason in the garrison of Fort Sumter. One story that was gravely published in a New York City newspaper, from the pen of its "own correspondent," was too cruelly malignant for any intelligent writer to be guilty of. It was stated that one of Major Anderson's men had a relative in Charleston, with whom he leagued to betray the fort; but the conspiracy was discovered, and the traitor condemned to die. A boat was sent to the city to request the attendance of a priest to shrive a sick woman, whose real business, however, was to prepare the culprit for execution, and at sunrise, next morning, he was ignominiously hung.

It is pleasant to know that this heartless

slander gained but little credence; and we would just say to the ingenious fabricator—we do not know him, but he knows himself, and he will see this—

Open your Bible—if you have not one borrow it—look for the 20th chapter of the book of Exodus, and carefully read the 16th verse.

Since the garrison had entered the fort a great deal had been done in strengthening its defences, and improving its capacities. One side of the fortress was weaker than the others. Not having been built with reference to any but foreign foes, of course that side of the wall which looked homeward, had been raised with less attention to resistance and security than the outer ones. This, under present circumstances, was a serious defect, and the very first to be remedied, as far as remedy was in the power of the occupants. Every man labored with energetic good-will. Their materials were turned to the most beneficial account, and some inventions of the officers attested a decided genius for overcoming difficulties.

Of the effectiveness of their weapons they

had no doubt, and only longed for an opportunity to let their neighbors know it also. One day, about the 1st of February, the weather being extremely fine, the Revolutionists turned out for a grand parade and drill. The little garrison saw from their walls the gay display in the city; and the Major, wishing to gratify his men, ordered one of his columbiads, shotted with explosive ball, to be run out and fired. The report startled the bold recruits ashore; and when the ball struck the water close by the wharf, sending spray to the house-tops, and raising foam for hundreds of yards around, the consternation was amusing to witness.

Through the interference of the President of the Southern Confederacy, Fort Sumter was again supplied with marketing, and comparative comfort was experienced within its walls.

The commission upon which Colonel Hayne and Lieutenant Hall had gone, in company, to Washington, had not succeeded. The Administration peremptorily refused to surrender Fort Sumter, or to yield one inch to the seceding cause.

On the 10th of February Lieutenant Hall

returned to the fort, bearing much information to his commander of the purposes of Government and the sentiment of the Union party throughout the country. But with political affairs that isolated band had nothing to do: they had but one duty, to hold the trust committed to them, or to resign it with their lives.

Great concern was spread through the garrison when, a few days after, Major Anderson was prostrated by sickness. His strength, of both mind and body, had been taxed to the utmost during the last few months—it had given way at last. The alarm of the company magnified the misfortune, and exaggerated their beloved leader's danger. What if the enemy should seize this opportunity of attacking them? Their officers were all brave and competent men; but *who* could fill the Major's place? and grave looks and muttered fears echoed "WHO?"

The anxiety communicated itself to the company's surgeon, Dr. Crawford, and caused him to desire a consultation. There was no apprehension of *his* skill being insufficient for the case; yet his wish was granted, a physician was summoned from Charleston, which circumstance furnished food to the hungry pen of every "own correspondent" in the city. Ere their labored communications appeared in print, however, the gallant Major was on his feet again, and his fellow soldiers rejoicing in his restoration to health.

February 22nd. This honored anniversary was celebrated with all due respect at Fort Sumter; and the thirty-four guns composing our national salute, loudly reverberated over the waters and made the houses of Charleston tremble.

In a few days a floating battery, which the Revolutionists had been constructing, was launched with much ostentation; but those whom it was intended to intimidate only smiled at its awkward appearance. It careened helplessly, and floundered about with a stupid indifference to breeze or rudder, while its warring capacity, or incapacity, was of an equally imbecile character. With a smile each of the garrison turned from a survey of this big toy, one young fellow archly observing:

"When they get folks frightened with such

a silly threat as that, it won't be the men of the gallant First."

So many reports had been circulated of treason among the soldiers of Fort Sumter that the subject had now become stale. An altered edition must, therefore, be got out, and, one day, the Charleston Mercury published the following.

"NOT IMPROBABLE.—It was currently rumored upon the streets yesterday that Major Anderson, and Lieutenants Davis and Talbott, of the garrison of Fort Sumter, would, on the 4th instant, resign their commissions in the United States army, and retire from the fort."

Well done, Madam Rumor! you capped the climax that time. If there is anything about your ladyship to be admired it is your audacity. And the temerity with which you state your most monstrous lies is only equaled by your unconsciousness of the utter contempt you excite in every honest mind!

Yet was it not malice alone that instigated the framing of this last slander: there was a subtle motive in the act. Major Anderson and Mr. Talbott were both Kentuckians, and Mr.

Davis from the neighboring State of Indiana;—it was expedient to make it appear that the Southern Confederacy would be largely augmented on the 4th of March, and what more valuable auxiliaries could they receive than brave and distinguished officers of the American Army? who more likely to sympathize with them than Southern and Western men? scatter amongst the people, then, the news—to the encouragement of the Secessionists, to the dismay of the Union party—that such names as Anderson, Talbott and Davis were to glitter on the rebel list.

Of the American officers who did resign their commissions on the 4th of March, we shall mention Peter G. T. Beauregard, for with him we have to do. He immediately went over to the revolutionary army, was appointed Brigadier General of the forces in and around Charleston, and from henceforth was the acting power, against whose sagacity and experience Major Anderson had to contend.

This man, when in the United States Army, had been connected with the Engineer Department, and had actually been engaged in *the building of Fort Sumter.* He knew, therefore, its strength and its capacity, was acquainted with its interior arrangements, and understood the nature of the facilities which its commander could bring to bear upon him. Of this knowledge he made good use in the planting of his batteries and the division of his troops; and it was easy to see, as we looked out from our isolated post, on the preparations going on around, that it was no stranger foe who was arrayed against us, but a deserter from our country's standard.

But the Major was on the alert, calm, watchful, resolute, no movement of the enemy escaping his observation, no counteracting resource forgotten or overlooked. He was prepared for any emergency; and the strong, firm expression of brow, eye and lips told that the soul of a warrior dwelt within that small, slender frame.

On the 11th of March a shot was fired from Cumming's Point, which struck the docking outside Fort Sumter. Major Anderson immediately made ready to reply to this demonstration, but scarcely were three of his embrasures open when a boat was seen approaching with a white flag, the mission of which was to apologize to the Commander of Fort Sumter for the accidental shot, which had been fired, the officer alleged, through mistake. Whether it was really a mistake, or was done with the design of testing the promptness of the Island fortress it is hard to say; but, in either case, of the latter fact convincing proof was given.

All through the month of March the little garrison lived quietly and worked steadily. In spare hours they read the papers, and talked enthusiastically of what they, each, could achieve, in honor of their flag, when permitted to put forth their strength. They troubled their heads little about politics in general; it was enough for them to know that the UNION was assailed, and the Nation threatened with disruption.

"I 'll tell you what it is, boys," said one of the privates, as he lounged on a bench in the yard, in the midst of a group of comrades, at the close of the day, "Government may be very wise in havin' patience with these fellows:

lettin' them seize national property through the country, an' makin' *us* sit still while they 're buildin' batteries all round us, to be used in attackin' ourselves; but I don't see the good-nature in all this patience, the fools will have to be brought back to their senses, and the sooner it 's done the better."

"You 're right in one sense," was replied by a sober looking man with a pipe in his mouth, "but may be Government 's waiting for them to do something treasonable, an' it 'll be easy to 'bring them to their senses' when the country goes about it."

"Treasonable!" exclaimed the first speaker, not heeding the closing remark, "I 'd like to know if they hav' n't done enough that 's treasonable already;—why, what is their Confederacy but one big treason?"

"It would be in your country," was the calm rejoinder, "where a man can be tried for his life for saying a word against king or government; but there 's more freedom here, and nothing less than taking up arms against the country constitutes treason."

"More 's the pity then!" said the Irishman,

earnestly, "I believe in liberty of speech, but if a disaffected faction can get up and band troops, seize Government property, supply themselves with guns and ammunition, and build batteries, and yet not be guilty o' treason—why—they 've more freedom than 's good for them; that 's what I say!"

"Tat 's so!" exclaimed a solid built German, with an oath, as he rose to his feet, "an' if ever ter was treason, it 's in tis harbor now; but if te Major would only say te word we 'd soon blow te treason out o' te tam rascals if te were twice as many!"

"I agree with you that, few as we are, we would be able to teach them a lesson," said he who had replied to the first speaker, "but the Major 's as ready to be at them as any of us—he 's only waiting for them to strike the first blow."

This man was right: the Major knew what he was doing. He saw that the crisis was approaching, and went on with stout heart to meet it. It came at last.

Toward the 1st of April the storage provisions had become so reduced in Fort Sumter that Major Anderson, in order to economize in that particular, arranged to send away the laborers employed in the fort; the State Authorities, however, refused to suffer them to depart. Of this interference with his movements and the circumstance preceding—namely, the reduction of his stock of provisions—the Major deemed it wise to apprise his Government; he, therefore, sent Lieutenants Talbott and Snyder with a flag of truce to Charleston, the former, by courtesy of the Governor, to proceed to Washington with dispatches. After the officers went ashore, and pending the return of Lieutenant Snyder to the boat, the men who rowed it took the opportunity of procuring tobacco and some other luxuries, but the police followed them and seized their purchases. This was on the 4th of April, and in two days after an order was issued by the State prohibiting the garrison of Fort Sumter any further supplies from Charleston Market.

Lieutenant Talbott made the journey to Washington and back in as short a time as possible; but on his return to Charleston he was refused permission to go to Fort Sumter. He, accordingly, returned immediately to Washington. The instructions to Major Anderson, of which he was the bearer, were, however, forwarded to the fort, and duly received there. They informed the Major that Government would immediately send him a supply of provisions, but as to the course he should pursue, they referred him entirely to his own judgment, expressing the utmost confidence in his bravery and military tact.

Upon this visit to Washington Mr. Talbott received promotion to a Captaincy, and, by the very next train for Charleston, returned thither as escort to Mr. Chew, a special messenger from the President to the Governor of South Carolina.

Mr. Chew's message was to inform Governor Pickens that it was the intention of the Government to send provisions to Fort Sumter, which would be landed there peaceably if permitted, but, if not, would be landed by force. This message was delivered on the 8th of April, and, after its delivery, Captain Talbott and Mr. Chew returned to Washington without delay.

Captain Talbott sincerely regretted his absence from Fort Sumter in this her hour of need. He knew the crisis had come, and that a sharp, severe struggle was before the gallant garrison, and, O! how he chafed under the necessity which compelled him away from the glory of sharing it with them.

The garrison was now on the look-out for the expected supplies, which must reach in a few days or not enter. The cause was this. Several weeks before the Carolinians had blocked the ship channel, by sinking the hulls of large vessels therein, leaving only a narrow passage, through which skillful piloting was necessary to lead large ships into harbor. The Charleston pilots had been forbidden by their State Government to steer into port any vessel bearing the United States Flag; it would, therefore, be impossible for the fleet to enter except during a very high tide, which would occur on the 10th and 11th of the month. Before that time, however, a storm arose which drove the vessels back; and when they at last arrived, it was too late—they could not enter.

Meanwhile they were expected; and the South Carolina authorities concluded to hurry up matters before their arrival. Accordingly, at two o'clock on Thursday, April 11th, a formal demand was sent by General Beauregard to Major Anderson for the evacuation of Fort Sumter. The Major's reply was as follows:

"SIR:—I have the honor to acknowledge the receipt of your communication, demanding the evacuation of this Fort, and to say in reply thereto that it is a demand with which I regret that my sense of honor and my obligations to my Government prevent my compliance.

"ROBERT ANDERSON."

The reception of this answer was immediately followed by a deputation from General Beauregard urging Major Anderson to evacuate, and proposing the most honorable terms, upon which he should be allowed to do so; but the Major, feeling his own strength, besides expecting the fleet from Washington, determined to hold out, and the deputation, after a long interview, in which they earnestly sought to persuade the Major to accept the offered terms, returned to Charleston to report their failure.

It was late on Thursday night when this interview closed; and at half past three o'clock, on Friday morning, the boat with its white flag, shrouded in darkness and mist, again drew up to the walls of Fort Sumter. It conveyed three of General Beauregard's Aid-de-camps, bearing the following notice:

"*Major Anderson*:

"By virtue of Brigadier General Beauregard's command, we have the honor to notify you that he will open the line of his batteries on Fort Sumter in one hour from this time."

Punctual to the minute, at half past four o'clock, the first gun was fired on Fort Sumter.

It was a dark, cloudy morning, not a star was visible, while a heavy mist covered earth and sea; but as through the sombre gloom came the brilliant flash of exploding shells from the batteries all around the bay, while the deep hoarse tones of talking cannon echoed over the waters, the scene was sublimely grand, and sensations wildly inspiriting swelled in every heart.

Major Anderson alone was calm, though the swollen veins of his temples, the dilating nostrils, the nervous lip, told that his great heart beat as ardently as any there.

He would allow of no hurry: he wished that his command should husband their strength as it would all be needed. With this view he desired that they should breakfast before proceeding to action.

Their simple meal was soon prepared. For a week they had been on short rations of salt pork, biscuit and coffee, with a little rice. This rice, the last they had received, had reached them through a rough sea, and, the boat being leaky, had become saturated with salt water. It had then been spread out in an empty room of the barracks to dry, with the expectation of its being very acceptable when the biscuit should give out. That extremity was reached now. The last few biscuits were divided, and the cook was ordered to boil some rice; but, lo! the very first fire had shattered the windows of the room where the precious article was spread, and particles of glass were thickly strewn amongst the grain—the food was useless.

But they still had a little pork and plenty of coffee; and, thankful for this same, the brave fellows eat and drank, then filed in order to their places in the casemates.

And all this time the enemy's shot rattled, thick and fast, around our stronghold, which did but little execution beyond affording the Major an opportunity of observing the efficiency of each battery employed against him, and of tracing the plan which he had to oppose.

At five o'clock day began to break; but the heavy masses of clouds which obscured the sky, the sullen swell of the dark waters, the grey mist which hung, like a sombre veil, over nature's face, only became more apparent as the gathering light increased.

Shortly after the huge clouds burst, and a deluge of rain rushed down upon the scene, as if commissioned to quench the matricidal fire leveled against Columbia's breast. But all in vain. The moaning wind—the splashing shower were scarcely heeded, or made but feeble sounds, while the hoarse bellowing of deep-mouthed cannon still rolled fiercely on. An hour, and the elements ceased to strive, the wailing storm was hushed, and a still but troubled sky looked down upon the scene.

Meanwhile the Fort Sumter garrison coolly prepared for action. Major Anderson divided his command into three reliefs of four hours each, for service at the guns; the first under charge of Captain Doubleday, assisted by Dr. Crawford and Lieutenant Snyder; the second under charge of Captain Seymour, assisted by Lieutenant Hall; and the third under charge of Lieutenant Davis and Lieutenant Meade. The laborers, over forty of whom were in the fort, were appointed to carry ammunition, help make cartridges and assist the gunners where their aid could be available.

All was now ready, every man was in his place, and still, before giving the word to fire, our kind commander walked around to administer his last charge.

"Be careful," he said, "of your lives; make no imprudent exposure of your persons to the enemy's fire; do your duty coolly, determinedly and *cautiously*. Indiscretion is not valor; reckless disregard of life is not bravery. Manifest your loyalty and zeal by preserving yourselves from injury for the continued service of our cause; *and show your love to me by guarding all your powers to aid me through this important duty.*"

This admonition, delivered in sentences, with anxious brow and broken voice, will long be remembered by those who heard it:—no doubt it was the fulcrum sustaining and steadying the power which cast such deadly force from Sumter's walls.

It was just within ten minutes of seven o'clock when the order was given to fire. The first shot was from a forty-two pounder directed against the battery at Cumming's Point. Three of our guns bore upon this point and seven on Fort Moultrie. The famous floating battery—which, by the way, did not float at all, but stuck fast on a point of Sullivan's Island—also received some attention, besides a new battery in the same neighborhood, which had only been unmasked the day previous.

Before our firing commenced—when the storm had cleared off sufficiently to enable us to see around us—we discovered a fleet, which we supposed to be our long-expected succor, outside the bar. The Major signaled them, but the shoals being heavy and the tide low, they could not possibly cross. Shortly after this a fragment of a shell struck and cut through one the flag halliards; but the flag, instead of falling, rose on the wind, and, with a whirl, flung the remaining halliard round the topmast, by which it was held securely all day:—Long live our gallant ensign!

To return. Major Anderson having opened fire continued to pour it forth with good effect. Almost every ball went home. One of the Fort Moultrie guns was soon disabled; the roofs and sides of the building were penetrated by shot; the flag-staff was struck and the flag cut. The floating battery was struck seventeen times; its roof was penetrated, and several shots were sent square through it. The iron battery at Cumming's Point was struck several times, but not much impression was made. Two of its guns, however, were dismounted. The forty-two pound Paixhans of our lower tier worked well: not one of them opened her mouth without giving the enemy cause to shrink, while the ten-inch Columbiads of our second tier meant every word they said. The barbette guns were not manned. Early in the engagement three of them had been fired; but the number of shells descending upon the terre-plain of the parapet, and the flanks and faces of the work being taken in reverse by the enemy's batteries rendered the danger of serving in the ramparts so imminent that Major Anderson quickly withdrew his men from them, and kept them in the casemates.

When the cartridges became scarce, the men not engaged at the guns were employed to make them; the sheets and bedding from the hospital being brought out and used for that purpose.

Noon came, yet Fort Sumter was not hurt: the proud stronghold had resisted every effort to do it serious injury. A new species of attack, however, was now resorted to. The solid pile which was impervious to cold ball might feel the influence of *hot shot*, especially as the barracks were constructed mainly of timber; and so a red, hissing shower rushed from Fort Moultrie on this treacherous errand.

The officers' quarters soon caught fire;—the roof of this elegant building, being taller than those adjoining, received the assault first, but the bursting of the cistern, on top, which occurred about the same time, prevented the conflagration from spreading. Still down came the fierce hot shot upon the doomed dwellings, and were it not for the leaking cisterns, each of which had been perforated by ball, the whole would have been quickly consumed.

The ball from the enemy's batteries continued to rattle against the fort, and the latter paid back the compliment with interest. A strong, determined will actuated our men, astonishing to find in so small a number, surrounded and hemmed in by an armament of thousands.

"Aye! there 's a great crowd o' them against us!" exclaimed one, as he leaned for a minute behind the column of an embrasure, "but it 's the Republic they 're fightin'—not us—and, in the name of the Republic, we 're able for them."

"To be sure we are!" was the hearty response, "seventy true men to seventy thousand traitors, and the true side is the strongest!"

And at it they kept, loading and firing, firing

and re-loading, without stopping for food or repose, except an occasional draught of coffee, to wash the powder from their throats, or a short rest for their weary shoulders against an arch or column.

Nor, all through the exciting day, did the officers ever flag in their duty. Cool, firm, and intrepid, with eyes like eagles, ears quick to hear, and limbs of agile motion, they saw every movement of the enemy, heard their leader's lightest command, and directed each action of their charge with a promptness and energy worthy the important occasion.

The day seemed short, too, full as it was with labor and excitement; and the hearts which beat with hope and enthusiasm heeded not the flight of time. They would fain fight on after day had closed; but the sun went down in lowering gloom, night gathered over us murky and chill, and Major Anderson ordered the firing to cease, and the men to eat some supper and to go to bed.

The only supper they had was a little pork and coffee; but this, with a good sleep, would afford them some refreshment, preparatory to the next day's toil; so they took it cheerfully and laid down.

Still the enemy's fire continued. Even when, at seven o'clock, a mighty storm arose, and rain descended with the force of a cataract, an occasional bomb from one of the batteries mingled with the fury of the elements, as if bidding defiance to nature as well as law.

The condition of the fort was now examined, and the injuries sustained were found to be as follows: The crest of the parapet had been broken in many places; the gorge had been struck by shell and shot, and some of these had penetrated the wall to the depth of twelve inches. Several of the barbette guns had been injured; one had been struck by a ball and cracked; one was dismounted and two had been thrown over by a recoil. The lower casemates were uninjured, save one or two embrasures a little broken on the edges.

But the internal structure had received the most damage—the *wooden* building which had been treated to hot shot. Nothing saved it from being consumed but the riddling of the cisterns which sent the water flowing after the fire as fast as the red balls kindled it; and now the copious rain came down to quench every spark that might have remained in wall or roof.

Yet the pretty edifice was in a sad condition: between fire and water our pleasant quarters were spoiled.

And here we would say, in parenthesis, to military engineers: Never use timber to build the barracks of a fort, nor raise the roof of your officers' quarters higher than the outer wall, unless you calculate upon deserting your colors, turning traitor to your cause, and heading a host in attacking that very fort. In such case you will find that having used that material will serve your purpose—as did Beauregard.

That we should be again saluted with hot shot was pretty certain, and, the cisterns empty and the rain storm over, nothing could save the wood works from destruction. As much of the officers' effects as could be removed, were, therefore, carried to the casemates—the privates, many of whom were now sleeping soundly in their barracks, had not much to lose.

The next morning rose fair and mild. The rain clouds had discharged their burden, and now a clear, calm sky looked down upon the scene. As day broke the firing from the enemy's batteries was resumed, and our garrison arose and prepared to reply to them. The meagre breakfast of pork and coffee was again partaken, and at seven o'clock Fort Sumter opened fire, which was kept up vigorously during the remainder of the contest.

The first few shots directed at Fort Moultrie sent the chimneys off the officers' quarters, and considerably tore up the roof; nearly a dozen shots penetrated the floating battery below the water line, and several of the guns on Morris Island were disabled. The clear state of the atmosphere to-day enables us to see some of the effects of our fire upon the enemy—*all* the effects we do not expect ever to learn.

As anticipated, hot shot was fired again from Moultrie upon the doomed buildings inside Fort Sumter; and at a little after eight o'clock the officers' quarters were ablaze. All the men, not on duty at the guns, exerted themselves to extinguish the fire, but it spread rapidly, igniting here and there, as the red balls continued to drop, until every portion was in flames.

Attention was now directed to the magazines, which were situated at each of the southern corners of the fort, between the officers' quarters and the barracks. An intimacy with the internal arrangements of the fort had, doubtless, suggested to the gentleman in the opposite command the possibility of blowing up the garrison—hence the clever stratagem of firing the officers' quarters with hot shot; but against this danger Major Anderson provided by ordering all the powder to be taken from the upper magazines, and the lower magazines to be shut tight and thick mounds of earth to be heaped round the doors, through which no amount of heat could penetrate.

Afterwards, when the fire had spread through the barracks and reached the casemates, the Major ordered the powder, which had been removed thither from the magazines, to be thrown into the sea, and ninety barrels were thus disposed of.

As the fire increased the situation of the garrison was distressing beyond description. The water from the cisterns, followed by floods of rain, had saturated the riddled and broken buildings so that they burned with a hissing, smoldering flame, sending forth dense clouds of vapor and smoke, which soon filled the whole fort, rendering it difficult to breathe. The men were often obliged to lie down in the casemates, with wet cloths over their faces, to gain temporary relief.

Still the valiant fellows continued to serve their guns, and bomb after bomb, resounding from Sumter's walls, told that the spirit of American loyalty was not to be subdued, even by fire.

About half past twelve o'clock our flag-staff, which had been grazed several times, was shot through and the flag fell. Down, amid burning brands, surrounded by smoke and ruin, our war-worn ensign lay.

It was but a moment, and the next our young Lieutenant, Mr. Hall, rushed through the fire and, dashing all impediments out of his way, seized the prostrate colors. A buzz of admiration, mingled with words of fear for the officer's safety, and every man started forward, straining his eyes through the smoke until the object of quest emerged to view, begrimed with soot, choking and faint, his face and hair singed, his clothes scorched, and holding aloft, with almost spent strength, the rescued flag. A weak, but heartfelt cheer, from parched throats, greeted him as the precious burden was taken from his blistered hands, and he sunk down exhausted.

When the fire was all spent, the gay dwelling in ashes, and the noble fort was silent—standing, proud as ever, in stern, strong nakedness—Mr. Hall's epaulets were found on the spot from which he had raised the flag. In rushing through the fire they had become heated, and, oppressing his shoulders, he tore them off. They were now burnt—all but one little bunch of gold wire, which was embedded in ashes. That little relic is in the writer's possession; treasured as one of the precious trifles belonging to History's store-house.

In fifteen minutes from the fall of the flag it was up again; a jury-mast was hastily raised, to which it was nailed, and it floated out as before. The honor of nailing it up belongs to

Mr. Peter Hart, a New York gentleman, who had come to Fort Sumter some time before, to visit Major Anderson, with whom he had served in the Mexican war, and had remained at the fort as his guest. Though he took no part in the actual battle, yet he made himself useful to the garrison in many ways, of which this, recorded, is not the least.

And still the fire raged within and the cannon roared without. The flames increased in strength and volume, the air became heated all through the fort; but the more the little garrison suffered the harder they fought, and each ball that flew from their embrasures performed its errand well.

At about half past one P. M. a boat was seen approaching from Cumming's Point. Arrived at Fort Sumter a gentleman sprang from it, and, with a white handkerchief tied to the point of his sword to represent a flag of truce, he ran up to a port-hole, which he entered, saying to a soldier, whom he met,

"I wish to see the commandant—my name is Wigfall, and I come from General Beauregard."

The soldier went to inform Major Anderson, and Mr. Wigfall passed into the casemate where he met Captain Foster and Lieutenant Davis. To them he also introduced himself, stating that he came from General Beauregard. Then he added excitedly:

"Let us stop this firing. You are on fire, and your flag is down—let us quit!"

Mr. Davis replied,

"No, Sir, our flag is not down. Step out here and you will see it waving over the ramparts."

He ran out and looked up, but the smoke filled his eyes and he exclaimed, impatiently extending his sword:

"Here 's a white flag,—will any body wave it out of the embrasure?"

Captain Foster said one of the men might do so, and Corporal Bingham, who was present, took it in his hand and jumped into the embrasure. And so the first white flag that waved from Fort Sumter was Senator Wigfall's handkerchief, tied to the point of that gentleman's sword!

But the firing still continued, when Mr. Wigfall said:

"If you will show a white flag from your ramparts, they will cease firing."

Captain Foster replied:

"If you request that a white flag shall appear there while you hold a conference with Major Anderson, and for that purpose alone, Major Anderson may permit it."

Major Anderson, at that moment came up, and the white flag was ordered to be raised.

"Major Anderson," said Mr. Wigfall, "you have defended your flag nobly, Sir. You have done all that is possible for man to do, and General Beauregard wishes to stop the fight. On what terms, Major Anderson, will you evacuate this fort?"

"Terms?" said Major Anderson, raising himself to his full hight, and speaking with emphasis, "*I shall evacuate on the most honorable terms, or—die here!*"

Mr. Wigfall inclined his head;—respect for the glorious soul in that slight, frail form could not be withheld by even an enemy.

"Will you, Major Anderson," he then asked,

"evacuate this fort upon the terms proposed to you the other day?"

"On the terms *last proposed* I will," was the reply.

"Then, Sir, I understand that the fort is to be ours?"

"On those conditions *only*, I repeat."

"Well, Sir, I will return to General Beauregard," said Mr. Wigfall; and, bowing low, he retired.

The white flag was then hauled down, and the American flag run up.

The Major now ordered that the firing should not be renewed, but that the men should take such refreshment as they had and rest awhile. Poor fellows! they were nearly exhausted. Those who had not been engaged at the guns had been toiling to subdue the fire; and faint for lack of food, and suffocating with smoke, it was only their giant hearts sustained them through.

When the flames were at the highest the enemy blazed away the faster, in order to cut down the men who were working to extinguish the fire; but a Divine shield was over them, and *not one life of the gallant First was taken by traitor hands.*

Some "own correspondent" stated that the Major sent men outside the fort on a raft to procure water wherewith to quench the fire :— nonsense! there was plenty of water inside for the purpose, if there had only been hands enough to use it; but the guns must be kept manned, so only those who could be spared from that duty gave attention to the burning buildings.

Their exertions, however, were sufficient to prevent explosions and disaster to life. The fire was kept under, and prevented from communicating with the magazines, until every ounce of powder was removed out of our reach also, for, when hostilities ceased, we had but four barrels and three cartridges on hand.

But the fire had done its work, and was now gradually burning out. The barracks and officers' quarters were destroyed; and as the smoke thinned away, so that the eye could penetrate the scene, nothing but charred and smoldering ruins were visible.

About three o'clock P. M. a formal deputation came to Major Anderson from General Beauregard and Governor Pickens, proposing the same terms as had been previously offered, except that they were not willing the Major should salute his flag.

To this Major Anderson would not consent.

About six o'clock came another deputation, consisting of Colonel Prior, Colonel Miles, Major Jones, and Captain Hartstein, and presented to Major Anderson General Beauregard's final terms. They were as follows. The garrison to march out with their side and other arms, with all the honors, in their own way and at their own time; to salute their flag and take it with them, and to take all their individual and company property; the enemy also agreeing to furnish transports, as Major Anderson might select, to any part of the country, either by land or water.

With all this Major Anderson was satisfied except the last clause. He would not consent to accept traveling accommodations from the enemy beyond the use of a steam-tug to convey him to the Government vessels outside the bar.

Outside the bar!—Oh! if they had been *inside*, what a different tale could the writer have told to-day!

This fleet comprised three steam transports, two sloops-of-war, one cutter and two steam-tugs. Had they been able to enter, and pour their men and provisions into Fort Sumter, the Stars and Stripes would be waving from its ramparts now. With enough men to work water upon the falling hot shot while enough remained at the guns, and with sufficient food to sustain them in their labors, under such a commander as Major Anderson, that fortress would have held out against a million foes.

As before mentioned, on their way down they were met by a storm which drove them back and separated them. One of the transports, the Baltic, and the cutter, Harriet Lane, reached Charleston Harbor on Friday morning, but late for the high tide. In attempting to enter, the Baltic ran aground on a shoal, and was with difficulty got off. She then lay to, waiting for the steam-tugs; but they had been blown out to sea, and did not arrive until after the evacuation, and the other transports were not seen.

On Saturday the sloops arrived, and, failing the appearance of the tugs, they determined to force an entrance that night. All this time a strong gale was blowing, against which they, with difficulty, bore up; but, though seven miles distant, they heard the firing, and longed to get to the succor of the garrison.

With the intention of appropriating a tug, the Harriet Lane chased a guard steamer into the harbor, but did not succeed in overhauling her. At last they seized a pilot, whom they induced, under promise of a large reward, to aid them; but just then the firing ceased, and they felt that all they could do for Major Anderson and his little garrison now was to carry them away.

All this we did not know while we were *within* Fort Sumter—we learned it afterwards; but we *did* know the condition of the harbor—the entrance encumbered with shoals, and even the narrow channel rendered still narrower by sunken hulls. We also knew that a storm was raging along the coast, and the entrance of large vessels, unless very skillfully piloted, was not only dangerous, but impossible.

It was this knowledge which necessitated the evacuation. As long as there was any hope of being enabled to maintain his post Major Anderson would not quit it *upon any terms;* and even when that hope was dead, he did not relinquish the fort without exacting the most honorable conditions.

And now all was arranged according to the Major's dictation, nothing remained but for the garrison to pack their effects and prepare to depart. This occupied great part of the night, and the next morning a Charleston steamer was in attendance to convey them to the fleet. The baggage was placed on board, then the men were drawn up under arms, on the parade, and a portion told off, as gunners, to salute their flag.

And now came the last solemn ceremony, to end even more solemnly than we expected. The guns began to fire. One after another their loud voices rolled out upon the Sabbath air until fifty were counted, and then—an explosion, a cry, a rush, and every gun was silent. A pile of cartridges, containing eighty pounds of powder, had been laid inside the bomb-proof, on the parapet, convenient to one of the guns. Among these cartridges a spark had fallen, and while the guns were firing, and the soldiers cheering, the powder exploded, tearing the strong sheets of iron, of which the bomb-proof was composed, into fragments, and scattering them abroad like feathers, at the same time sending a shock—a thrill of horror to every heart, for a group of men had been standing round, and Oh! where were they now?

A few moments and anxious faces were gathered to the scene of the disaster:—sad scene!—one of our brave fellows was dead—quite dead—rent almost in two; another was dying—fractured in every limb; another yet so mutilated that the Doctor only shook his head, and six others more or less injured.

The departure of the garrison was, of course, delayed by this accident—the dead and the wounded must be caréd for; yet the process of evacuation must be concluded, and so, while with tender hands and moist eyes the soldiers removed their bleeding comrades, the flag, in vindicating whose honor this warm blood was spilt, drooped its proud pinions and slowly descended from the ramparts.

All that men in their circumstances could do was then done by the garrison for the dead and wounded: the former was prepared for decent burial, the latter tended with the kindest care.

The enemy, impatient to take possession of the fort, now arrived. Governor Pickens and General Beauregard with their aids landed and entered, but, seeing what had occurred, immediately tendered every assistance. A minister was accordingly sent for to Charleston, to perform the service for the dead, and physicians to take charge of those whom we should be obliged to leave behind living. Meanwhile a strong coffin was put together, a grave dug in the parade, and, shortly after the clergyman arrived, the funeral proceeded.

With military honors the scarcely cold remains were buried: the Major heading the procession with crape upon his sword. With the rites of the Church the coffin was lowered into the grave, and, awaiting the resurrection, when the justice of every cause shall be righteously proved, Daniel Howe was left sleeping in Fort Sumter.

The wounded men, all but two who were quite unfit to bear the voyage, were then removed to the steamer. These, under promise of the kindest treatment, were trusted to the hospitality of the South Carolinians; one of them, George Fielding was, therefore, conveyed to the Charleston Hospital, the other, Edward Galway, whose hours were numbered, was made as comfortable as possible in the fort.

These sad details arranged, Major Anderson issued his final orders for embarkation; and, carrying their flag and even its shattered mast, with band playing *Yankee Doodle*, the garrison marched out of the fort and went on board the steamer. As the Major emerged from the gate the music changed into *Hail to the Chief*:—simple tribute but no less heart-felt!

It was now late in the afternoon, and the garrison had eaten nothing since their scanty breakfast of pork and coffee; it would, therefore, have been most desirable to have got out on board the transport without delay; but the state of the tide was such that the little steamer could not move, and all night she lay under the walls of Fort Sumter. Had they had only their own discomforts to think of, they would have felt more the inconveniences of that long delay without food or resting places; but thoughts of their dying comrade in the fort, whose groans almost reached their ears, filled their minds, even to the exclusion of self. Before they left, however, the sufferer was released. An officer came on board the steamer to inform Major Anderson of the death of Edward Galway, and to assure him that the deceased should be buried beside Howe, with the honors due to a brave soldier.

Those two men, Daniel Howe and Edward Galway, were natives of Ireland—the first from the County Tipperary, the last from the County Cork. They fought in the defence of our flag, they died in doing it honor:—their blood was the first that flowed—their lives were the first that were sacrificed in the cause of our glorious UNION.

Early on Monday morning, April 15th, with the rising of the tide, the Isabel, on board which our garrison lay, steamed out of the Charleston waters to where the United States vessels lay, waiting to receive the gallant freight. The little band were welcomed with cheers by the fleet, and the Baltic, on board which they were taken, felt honored by their presence. Every preparation had been made for their comfort, and nothing that could be done to atone for their past privation was neglected.

The Sumter flag, which had floated over the Isabel, was immediately hoisted on the Baltic, and a salute fired; and then Major Anderson was observed to bow his head and weep.

What, tears? Yes, Reader, tears! We don't conceal the fact. Great men can *feel.* It was told of Xerxes—why not tell it of our own loved hero? He looked up at his flag, tattered and begrimed, yet free as ever; he looked round at his comrades, wan and weary, but with hearts of stoutest metal, and emotion mastered him—he bowed his head and wept.

The Baltic was soon under weigh; and, after a pleasant run of three days reached Sandy Hook, where she was boarded by the Medical Staff from Staten Island, and quite a crowd of gentlemen who had come in boats, from New York, to meet her.

Here Major Anderson wrote the following dispatch to the War Department.

"STEAMSHIP BALTIC, off SANDY HOOK,
"Thursday, April 18, 1861.

"*Hon. S. Cameron, Secretary of War, Washington, D. C.:*

"SIR:—Having defended Fort Sumter for thirty-four hours, until the quarters were entirely burned, the main gates destroyed by fire, the gorge wall seriously injured, the magazine surrounded by flames, and its door closed from the effect of the heat, four barrels and three cartridges of powder only being available, and no provisions but pork remaining, I accepted terms of evacuation, offered by General Beauregard, being the same offered by him on the 11th instant, prior to the commencement of hostilities, and marched out of the fort, Sunday afternoon, the 14th instant, with colors flying and drums beating, bringing away company and private property, and saluting my flag with fifty guns.

"ROBERT ANDERSON,
"Major First Artillery."

It was a bright, sunny day as the Baltic steamed up New York Harbor, saluted by the firing of cannon from the forts, and by the ringing of bells and waving of flags from the city as she approached. The late garrison of Fort Sumter was drawn up on her quarter-deck, considerably restored in appearance by good food and rest; and the Major, surrounded by his officers, stood on the wheel-house, still looking pale and care-worn, his expressive features quivering with emotion as he acknowledged the salutations of the people.

All is now told—as far as a hasty sketch can tell it—of what transpired within Fort Sumter: of the energy, courage and determined will which sustained that little garrison to the last. And now you talk of promoting Major Anderson:—*promote Major Anderson!*—Could you promote the lion among beasts—the eagle among birds? could you exalt Sorata among mountains, or dignify the Amazon among streams? could you give distinction to the North Star, or brighten the sun-beam? as well might you attempt to elevate one who has arisen on the pinions of his own grand spirit to the hilltop of glory. No, fellow-countrymen, *you can not promote Major Anderson!* You can give no higher rank to the premier of his contemporaries—you can confer no prouder title on the HERO OF CHARLESTON HARBOR.